Spain

Your Ultimate Guide to Traveling, Culture, History, Food and More!

By Jing Dalagan

Experience Everything Travel Guide Collection™

EXPERIENCE EVERYTHING
P U B L I S H I N G

Forward

Thank you for purchasing this book from the Experience Everything Travel Guide Collection™! Inside you will find a ton of useful and entertaining information on Spain and it is our desire that this book will provide you with the inspiration to explore!

Disclaimer

While this book contains a great deal of information, it does not have all of the information that is available on the Internet. It is written to inspire you about the destination rather than act as a full travel guide that you could use to get from point A to point B or to specific addresses/locations during your tour.

Contents:

Introduction

Spain is known in the media for matador bullfighting and flamenco dancers. Most tourists would go to Spain, apart from learning the Spanish language, to enjoy the parks, museums and cuisine. However, Spain is much more than that.

If ever there is a culture known for its pleasure-seeking tendencies like eating, drinking and partying, it would be the Spanish. Add siesta into the mix and you would realize how they take leisure time seriously. No wonder tourism is big business here!

Just a heads-up though about bullfighting, the Catalan Parliament, inspired by the law enforced in the Canary Islands in 1991, has officially banned bullfighting in their area - a clear contrast to how the said traditional sport is being given a cultural heritage status in other regions like Murcia, Valencia and Madrid. Their respective congressional districts are trying to legalize bullfighting's status for the sake of cultural heritage.

Then again, touring Spain is not limited to watching the matadors play with death in the form of a raging bull. From the tapas to paellas to museums, to the open parks and the nightlife that some major cities in Spain are known for, this guide will explore it all. Feel free to bring out that Spanish guitar and start playing along!

Chapter I: Geography

Located in southwestern Europe, Spain occupies the larger part of the Iberian peninsula. If you include the Canary Islands in the Atlantic, the Balearic Islands in the Mediterranean and territories in North Africa, it makes Spain the third largest state in all of Europe, just behind Russia and France. At the heart of Spain lies its capital, Madrid, 650 m above sea level.

If you'd like to locate Spain from space, you need to spot the Iberian peninsula in Europe. Protruding on the western corner of the European continent, Spain is roughly estimated at 492,000 square kilometers. Spain occupied about four-fifths of this peninsula and ended up becoming an attractive territory worth conquering when navigation was still a challenge in the high seas. It is more or less twice the size of the British Isles. In case you need a comparison that's easier to imagine, think of the land mass the size of the state of California plus a quarter of Nevada.

Spain's plain is better known among the locals as "la meseta", the area that occupied a chunk of Spanish topography surrounded by mountain ranges. The mountain ranges that would serve as walls or barriers between this plateau and the Mediterranean was the Pyrenees. In case the Pyrenees sound familiar to you, they often get mentioned in reference to the mountain ranges in the Spanish topography. But you don't call the entire mountain range as the Pyrenees. It's just part of the mountain range stretching from the Bay of Biscay to the Mediterranean, not the whole mountain range itself.

To the east and north of the Iberian mountains you can find the cities of Valencia, Cataluna, Aragon and Navarra. South the Iberian mountain range is where Andalucia is found. Go west and you end up finding yourself to the border between Spain and Portugal. Combing through "la meseta" and you will see the Cantabrian Mountains. The Cantabrian Mountains serve as a boundary for this plain.

Now since the northeastern part of the Iberian peninsula is mentioned, this leads to one of the prominent areas in Spain. That area is Catalonia just right on northeastern corner itself. Halfway along the peninsula coastline is Barcelona, the capital of Catalonia. This is the heart of the Catalan-speaking populace of Spain. Let this serve as a reminder to anyone traveling to Barcelona for the first time that not everyone in Spain speaks Spanish which is known to the locals as Castellano.

Going back to areas teeming with Spanish speaking people, the discussion then takes the curious towards the Canary Islands. This archipelago is found on the western side of Morocco lying on the Atlantic Ocean. It consists of seven islands - El Hierro, La Palma, La Gomera, Fuerteventura, Lanzarote, Tenerife and Gran Canaria. Much of the 2-million-strong populace that lived on this archipelago is found on the largest islands of Tenerife and Gran Canaria as well as economic activity. This archipelago is occasionally compared to Hawaii due to the presence of active volcanoes. Total land area is estimated at 7,447 sq km showcasing a nice array of flora and fauna.

Chapter II: History of Spain

While much of how Spain came to be is attributed to the history of the Iberian peninsula itself, the origins of Spain itself was traced after a cave was discovered with about 150 animals painted drawn on the walls. Archaeologists estimated the time these sketches were made depending on the found material used on them. The earliest sketches were found to be drawn with pieces of charcoal while the latter sketches were draw with pieces of animal fat and blood.

It was 1879 when these sketches were first discovered after a young girl mistook some of them for bulls. The sketches turned out to be bison, one of the animals usually associated with prehistoric records. This became what is known now as the Altamira Cave. Some artists have gone as far as calling it "The Sistine Chapel of prehistoric art" since the sketches may be prehistoric, but not primitive. Spain's ancestors turned out to be just as artistically inclined as some Spaniards today as these sketches were estimated to be drawn fifteen thousand years ago.

The sketches were met with skepticism until similar "paintings" were found in France years later. So art must have been a part of prehistoric culture in the Iberian peninsula even millenniums before.

This is a part of Spanish history that does not often gets mentioned as much of Spanish civilization is attributed to the Romans. For an empire that took two centuries to develop on the Iberians, it managed to instill its distinct architecture in cities like Segovia, Merida and Zaragoza. From amphitheater to theaters to bridges and even a 3,000 foot-long-strong Acueducto Romano in Segovia itself, Roman influence is very prominent. It serves as a concrete (pun intended) gateways to the past.

Much of the art often attributed to Spain today can easily be found on the architecture of buildings found in Spain.

Not just what you see in museums and gallaries, most of the time, the cathedral itself is the work of art. It reflects the various influences that Spanish architecture absorbed from its colonizers, the Moors during the Crusades, and from its European neighbors like France and Italy.

Most of the earliest works or architectural art date back to the 8th and the 13th centuries. These were the Romanesque churches. Distinct features include few windows, massive walls and round arches. Most of them are still found in the Catalonia region and are usually included in the itinerary when visiting this area.

For history enthusiasts with a need for deeper research about the Moor invasion of Spain around the same time, it's safe to say that this was during the time when religious wars still occurred in these areas. Just when the Visigoths have managed to annex away northern Spain away from the Roman Empire, the Moors invaded it, kicking the Visigoths out of the area. For about 800 years, the Moors ruled northern Spain under Islam and instilled their influence not just on architecture but on language and agriculture as well.

Moorish rule officially ended the moment the Catholic monarchs, Isabel and Ferdinand, secured their power in a union that helped secure the Church's hold on the country. Under their reign, Granada fell and the Crusades won. The kingdom wasted no time in installing churches that were highly influence with the Gothic architecture. It was the most prominent influence that France had on Spain. The Gothic style applied on the churches constructed on Granada and elsewhere in the Catholic territories earned the name Isabeline Gothic.

Isabeline Gothic architecture was the Catholic monarch's answer to the Moorish architecture that dominated these areas then. The Catholic monarch's army's defeat of the Moors is even illustrated on murals in some of the cathedrals of Granada. There are also carvings on the altar of some cathedrals illustrating stories from the New Testament.

Outside the cathedral, the Isabeline Gothic is evident through features like the flying buttress, tracery, rose window and the pointed arch. Designs were interchangeable but these features consistently appeared on the cathedrals.

Fast-forward to the 19th century and Spain bore witness to the Spanish Civil War. General Francisco Franco reclaimed Madrid from the Allied Forces. Aided by Germany's Condor legions and troop support from Italy, Franco's troops stormed their way to Madrid on March 27, 1939. The Nationalist forces ruled Spain then.

Chapter III: Culture

Spaniards are known for that zest in life. Friendly and accommodating, some of them have a real knack for hosting events and meeting new people. Some tourists find it amusing that dinner does not get served not until 9pm. Afternoons are usually spent enjoying their "siesta". That's their term for their cat nap. When it's hot and humid outside as it is mostly in Spain, time flies by more comfortably when it's rest time. The energy earned for that time would be enjoyed partying during "madrugada". That's the local term for the hours between midnight and dawn.

Eating together means a big group hanging out in a tapas bar and talking. Talking comes as naturally as eating and when they talk, it's a fun occasion where food and lively discussions are shared often talking over each other. The locals often find it easy to spot tourists and foreigners this way - when they don't talk because there are several people talking at the same time and they don't know who to listen to first. The locals will ask you politely why are you so quiet. Talking is their idea of community. Dinners and bar hopping become convenient excuses to gather and socialize.

Football, or Soccer as it's known in North America, is followed religiously in Spain. So you don't talk about FC Barcelona in Madrid unless you wanted to discuss how Real Madrid defeated them. It may be one of the most animated discussions to get into in one of those bar-hopping tours. So while getting to know people through chit-chat would be nice, don't forget to watch your words. Other sports commonly talked about would be tennis. If you're a fan of Rafael Nadal, the King of Clay himself, you would find kindred spirit among the cities here.

For a government with close ties to the Roman Catholic Church, there are cities where a nice balance between Christianity and Islam are found. Granada was one of the last Moor strongholds that fell to the army under Isabel and Ferdinand. Cordoba on the other hand was the main stronghold during the glory days of the Moor inquisition. Although much of the populace has gone secular, most of the architecture found in these cities are preserved for historical purposes.

Perhaps one of the main reasons why history is preserved well here in Spain is because artists had used history to base their artistry from. Architecture is not the only form where history can be seen and felt. When artists are honest enough to pour their commentary into their art, you feel the authenticity in staring at works by Francisco de Goya and El Greco. Most of them are found at the Reina Sofia Museum and the Prado Museum. These are just two of the museums to be discussed at length in the next pages to come.

Chapter IV: Getting Around

In Madrid, getting around by foot is normal. Most of the roads have been relocated underground. Same goes for the subway that offers cheap tickets. Locals can only tell you how hot it can get in the city that taking the subway train offers a cool mode of transportation. Just look for the underpass with the sign saying "Metro Sol" hanging on the arc to get into the subway. Learning a few Spanish words like "Salida" would help you get around. The word "Salida" is often found written on green signs that direct you to the subway exit.

Having a car to drive around nearby cities like Granada and Cordoba would be advisable if you would like to enjoy the scenery. Besides, while much of what made Spain attractive to tourists is the summer, it can get too hot for comfort. A reliable, air-conditioned rent-a-car service would be an nice, cool option.

Getting around by foot in other cities serves as a viable option too. In Sevilla, for example, since most shops are located beside each other, window shopping is the least chosen option. Buying a shawl or some "abanicos" or folding fans is highly recommended for the same sweltering heat that you need to manage when walking around the city.

Good thing in Barcelona, transport services are available to take you to various hot spots in the city. Trains are available here too apart from buses. Tourist packages get assembled to include such conveniences, letting you choice between travel agency-affiliated public transport or the rent-a-car service mentioned. Not just in Barcelona but in other cities as well.

In the evening, since the Spaniards party like there is no tomorrow, bar hopping comes easy. Add the modernized bars that play electronic dance music and contemporary house mixes and you realize that as much as Spain takes pride in its history, they enjoy looking forward to a fun-loving future. Whether you feel like trying the tapas bars in Madrid or the culinary hubs in Andalucia, having a tour guide or a friend that lived there would be advisable company.

Chapter V: Where to Stay

Just a disclaimer: the hotels mentioned here are just suggestions when it comes to places to stay the night. The typical basis for the suggestions here would be proximity to the airport or the tourist areas on your itinerary.

Madrid

Catalonia Atocha Hotel

Right in the heart of Madrid, this hotel is just half a kilometer away from the Atocha Railway station. As much as Madrid is still viewed as one of those rustic cities, reliant on old-school charm, walking around the halls of this hotel would confirm rumors of the city's inhabitants embracing modernity. It is the hotel worth recommending since siesta would mean most shops closed due to the sweltering heat that the locals have been trying to avoid. So when everything else, including the pharmacy, is closed, staying in the hotel to kill time comes easy. The airconditioning works well and flat screen TV would keep you and your family occupied until dinner. Do as the Romans do, so to speak, taking a few hours nap to wake up just in time for dinner.

TRYP Madrid Atocha Hotel

Now this is the hotel to go to if you prefer to embrace the old-fashioned Madrid you initially heard and read about. The 19th century building which this hotel is housed got preserved knowing there would be historians and romantics alike that would seek such features here in this city. Also, it's the hotel closest to Puerta del Sol and the museums, Museo del Prado and the Centro de Arte Reina Sofia. Walking tours would usually have this hotel as a landmark to start the trip with your chosen guide since almost in the same block, you can pass by Palacio Royal, Congress and Paseo de la Castellana.

Barcelona

Olivia Plaza Hotel

This is the hotel to spend the night or early morning, whichever comes first, if you see yourself bar-hopping around Barcelona. It's the hotel closest to Hard Rock Cafe, a good spot to start. If partying the night away is the goal here, at least you have landmarks worth remembering. Shopping areas are also close by for souvenirs and other trinkets. And this is the hotel closest to Las Ramblas, one of the top shopping destinations for Barcelona. Even if you come to this city for business purposes, there is no way you're going to miss the breath-taking views of gothic church of Santa Ana and the Plaza Catalunya. Enticing views supported by the ideal location with which this hotel is situated.

Catalonia Square Hotel Barcelona

Just like how the right hotel helped in finding starting points for the walking tours in Madrid, the same analogy can be applied here in Barcelona. This is just a 17-minute-drive away from the airport. With the hotel and the airport not far from each other, the top tourist destination are accessible such as the Palau de la Musica Catalana.

Valencia

Hotel Las Arenas

One of the hotels closest to the Malvarrosa Beach, exploring Valencia from this point is one of the best decisions you can make if you chose this city as your next destination. Choosing the right hotel whenever on a business or leisure trip helps when you plan on using your free time in strolling around the city. It helps that it is in close proximity with top-notch destinations like Ciudad de las Artes y Ciencias, the Oceanographic and, of course, the beaches.

Hotel Vora Fira

Now speaking of business trips, chances are some of the conferences held in Spain are held in Valencia, notably the Valencia Trade Fair Grounds. A few minutes away from Ciudad de las Artes y Ciencias, it is also one of the closest to the airport itself. True to its image as the hotel by the coast, Mediterranean cuisine is served in the restaurant on site. There are several places to eat in Valencia. But tourists chose this hotel not only for the superb accommodation but also for the food, in case they don't have enough time to go around the restaurants and try some paellas.

Seville

Vertice Sevilla

This hotel is found in that spot that serves as a residential and business district for the city otherwise known as "Sevilla" to locales. Driving from the San Pablo International Airport to this hotel only takes 15 minutes. Take your pick among 157 modern guestrooms here but book as early as possible knowing Seville is one of the high density areas among the cities in Spain. It is often the choice of hotel to stay into for folks traveling for business. It only takes a few steps from here to the Convention Center a.k.a. Palacio de Congresos. Very modern, it serves as a pleasant contrast to the rustic atmosphere that Seville has to offer.

Gran Melia Colon Hotel

A 5-star hotel recently refurbished to keep its service at high quality levels, it is found in Seville's old district. This establishment maintained the nostalgic Andalusian feel to complement the amenities that it modernized. It strikes a nice balance between the traditional Andalusian look and the modernized facilities. It is what made Seville a pleasant city to stay into especially when much of your itinerary relies on leisure. A sauna on-site is ready to accommodate you knowing that much about going around Seville involves walking and the restaurant on-site features traditional Andalusian cuisine.

Chapter VI: Where to Go and Where to Eat

Madrid

Museo del Prado

No matter how excited you are to see the works of Goya and El Greco inside, make sure to pick up a copy of the guide as you enter Museo del Prado. Occasionally mentioned in English language travelogues, Museo del Prado should be one of the first stops to make here in Madrid. By Spanish museum building standards, it is small. But it is packed with most of the classical art you need to see as a visual approach to learning Spanish history. The Spaniards take their history lessons seriously as you will realize by the artworks exhibited there. Whatever the painters could not write in history books, they illustrated in the paintings.

Centro de Arte Reina Sofia

Centro de Arte Reina Sofia is the museum tourists go to whether they have been serious art enthusiasts or casual spectators. Why would the art history buffs get here the soonest they arrive in Madrid? It serves as the sanctuary for Pablo Picasso artwork, one of the most influential artists of all time. The best way to understand that is by going straight to his best work yet - Gernika. When painters unleash their commentary on the canvas, it resonates in the images produced. So comparing the artworks here will give you an idea about the beliefs and convictions that the artists are trying to express. If you are the kind that takes arts really, really seriously, don't leave Spain without dropping by here.

Palacio Real de Madrid

In case the front facade of Palacio Real is familiar to you, it is because you may have seen in in some news outlets. It is the official residence of the Spanish Royal family. The square in this palace called Plaza de la Armeria contains the armory that has served as historical artifacts intended for display. It looks like a throwback to the days when Spain was a force to reckon with in the imperial wars. Most of the artifacts found here can be traced to the days of El Rey Felipe Segundo (King Philip II) and King Charles I of Spain a.k.a. Holy Roman Emperor Charles V. There are several more sections to the Royal Palace but viewing the armory is highly recommended. The Spaniards take pride in their accomplishments so much that you could feel it reflected on these imperial artifacts.

Where to Eat in Madrid

A tapas bar named Jose Luis is located in Calle Serrano close to the museums. The museums used to be 19th century mansions owned by Lazaro Galdiano and Joaquin Sorolla. The food served at Jose Luis though served as a pleasant contrast. A tapas platter contains salmon with capers and cream cheese, mini-Hamburguesa and tortilla. So imagine all of the influences infused in one platter alone. Having two or three friends with you would be good as tapas bars in Madrid would often serve the "racion" editions of the tapas (plates meant to be shared) to go with sangria.

Also on Calle Serrano is the Mallorca restaurant where Spanish gourmet dinners are served. Since Mallorca and Jose Luis are on the same street, you can have the tapas appetizers at Jose Luis first and dine at the Mallorca. Then off to bar-hopping in the metro. That is if you have gotten enough of the tapas served here. Best eaten with toasted bread and gazpacho sauce.

A few blocks from Calle Serrano is O'Caldino located in Lagasca 74. It's also a tapas bar but more traditional. Most of the dishes served here has that traditional Spanish cuisin feel like the polpo alla gallega and the cogote de merluza. Both dishes are more on the Mediterranean side having some seafood meat in them.

Now for restaurants within the same vicinity as that of Museo del Prado, worth mentioning is Restaurante El Botanico. A restaurant in the middle of the botanical garden, this is where you go for some coffee after walking those halls. It's more of a cafe than a restaurant that serves as a pit stop for a day reserved for touring the museums.

Lastly, since its places to eat close to Museo del Prado is sought here, do not miss the Goya restaurant. The chocolate arroz con leche that they serve here is the closest equivalent that they can offer to an oatmeal. Spanish style oatmeal is one of the best ways to start your tour. But in this case, it's also one of the best ways to cap it off. They also have paella that you can order on the get go before even looking what's on the menu.

Barcelona

Barri Gotic

The preserved Roman origins of Spain are found here at Barri Gotic (Gothic Quarter) and, as much as Barcelona, is one of the cities in Spain that is fun to stroll around in since it has a floor plan that would challenge your exploring skills. A little warning though in case you entertain that thought - it has become advantageous to certain pickpockets. Since lost tourists are the most vulnerable to them, travel in groups. Vehicles are allowed here but usually limited to taxis and privately-owned vehicles. Exploring the quarter for the sights would be great once you learned how to be careful as long as you have the cathedral as the landmark to remember.

Museu d'Historia de la Ciutat

Museu d'Historia de la Ciutat (Museum of the History of the City), MUHBA for short, often gets mentioned separately from Barri Gotic in travelogues. If ever Barcelona wanted to cut to the chase about introducing itself, it would present you MUHBA. This is where Barcino, the precursor of what Barcelona is today, is preserved in the form of Roman era artifacts. From domestic chores like doing the laundry to cottage industries like dying cloth, these artifacts present an era that looks at some of the daily chores done by Spanish ancestors that is still done in the city today.

La Seu

La Seu (The Cathedral) is one of the earliest constructions here in Barcelona traced to the 11th Century. It was more of a reconstruction since the Moors destroyed a chunk of this building when they invaded the city. And it still stands to this day. Entering La Seu will introduce you to the 29 side chapels here. That's more than twice the needed Visita Iglesia a Roman Catholic needed to complete the Voyage of the Cross during Semana Santa (Holy Week in the Vatican calendar). Apart from becoming a focal point for pilgrim tourists visiting Barcelona, it often served as the focal point of entrance for tourist groups when entering Barri Gotic.

Sagrada Familia

Occasionally referred to by tourists as THE Cathedral, Sagrada Familia causes some confusion for some tourists until they learn that much of the label attached to it is due to its stupendous size. Eventually, by virtue of the power bestowed on then Pope Benedict XVI, the church was elevated to a basilica. Even churches get promotions too and Sagrada Familia turned out to be one of the more prominent "non-human" cases of promotions. Much of the overall appearance of Sagrada Familia is based on the vision of Antoni Gaudi, the Catalan architect that designed this UNESCO world heritage site.

Where to Eat in Barcelona

Since shopping would be included in the itinerary here at Barcelona, the basis used in finding places to eat would be how close they are to Passieg de Gracia. Roco Bar, is a casual dining restaurant that serves Spanish cuisine and is an excellent place to rest after draining your energy at the shopping stalls with the mouth-watering desserts they can offer you.

Roca Bar is more of a tapas bar than a Mediterranean restaurant. And it's a joint to hop into with friends. The tapas served here is noted on the menu as "to share". In case you plan to hang out alone, just make sure to mention to the waiter that orders are for one. This way, you would avoid paying more than you can eat.

Another great establishment, Boca Chica is the place to go for some cocktails. Regular tourists often come back to Boca Chica whenever they have the opportunity. From interiors that let you stretch out after all that haggling during your shopping spree, unwind with their award-winning drinks - the gin/tonic combo "Infusion" and the Mediterranean cocktail "Bloody Sun".

If you have time for a full meal after Boca Chica, you can move over to Boca Grande, the bar's restaurant arm. Cocktails to go with your Mediterranean meal? Most certainly. You can expect tasty mixed drinks, fresh sea food, and a relaxing ambience all in one area.

Valencia

Las Torres de Serrano

Las Torres de Serrano (The Gateways of Serrano) are the most prominent landmarks here in Valencia. These towers are part of the defensive wall that once existed in the city as early as the 12th Century. For a city exposed along the coast, it became very attractive to conquerors and pirates alike. This landmark served as one of the best proofs of the efforts of the inhabitants to protect their city.

Torres de Quart

Another proof of the long-lasting mark of the defensive walls on Valencia, the Torres de Quart tower is just as imposing and prominent as Las Torres de Serrano. It is found on a different street serving as a focal point for the rest of the famous remnants of the wall that once protected Valencia.

Micalet

Better known as The Bell Tower, Micalet was constructed from the remnants of the defense wall in 1381 by Julia Andreu. A Gothic-inspired tower, it served as a home to several chapels that instilled the Roman Catholic religion in Valencia. The Holy Grail is the main attraction in this tower, located in one of the chapels inside.

Iglesia del Patriarca

A chapel in the historical quarter also in the same compound as that of the Gateways of Serrano, Torres de Quart and Micalet, this cathedral is also known by its other names "El Patriarca" and "Corpus Christi". Much of the historical quarter displayed Gothic and Baroque architectural influences. But this cathedral clearly exuded Baroque architecture dating back to the 16th and the 17th century. That influence is seen on the frescos that graced the vaults and walls here.

Ciudad de las Artes y las Ciencias

Ciudad de las Artes y las Ciencias (City of Arts and Sciences) is the most booked venue for business conferences. Cultural events locally and internationally are also held here, making the contemporary tourist attraction for corporate trips. It helped established Valencia as a modern city since, while the cathedrals, towers and chapels still attract tourists, it is this venue that helped stage successful business conferences. Events helped promote business and leisure in a city through state-of-the-art venues like this spot.

La Malvarrosa Beach

Since this is a Mediterranean city, might as well hit the beach. La Malvarrosa Beach is an open beach that stretches a full kilometer and is one of the highly recommended destinations here in Valencia. If you are going to enjoy summer by the beach here in Spain, bookmark La Malvarrosa Beach. Soak up the sun. Stroll by the seashore. Have fun. It's the Mediterranean for you to enjoy.

Where to Eat in Valencia

This list is based on the closest restaurants available in the City of Arts and Sciences. Vertical Restaurant is the place to go for good food to go with the ambiance. Dining in with a spectacular view of the city makes the crema de foie sweeter. It's their version of dulce de leche. If you like it fruity and sweet, they have desserts that contain chocolate, berries and cream with ingredients that made them healthier. Rice meals like the Arroz con acelgas and noodle meals like the Fideua would be highly recommended for folks that don't mind the carbs. The appetizers are bite-sized anyway so the bulk of the dining experience is enjoyed at the main course.

Trafalgar Bistro is a laid-back casual dining restaurant that balances three cuisines - Mediterranean, Spanish and tapas. Toasted verduras to go with cream cheese and toppings would start the meal early on a healthy note. Tomato soups like the salmorejo would be a filling main course. Bacon and cheese topped on soup never looked this good. Desserts like chocolate chip muffins and vanilla-ice cream-topped brownie pies are two of the choices available for you.

48 Restaurante & Copas looks like one of those soda pop shops you may have seen in the movies except that they serve Mediterranean and Spanish cuisine to go with drinks. Bar food worth recommending would be the scallops, beautifully presented in true Mediterranean fashion.

Seville

Real Alcazar

Real Alcazar serves as the royal palace and is a mash-up of influences between the Moor occupation and the "Reconquista" (reconquest) of Spain. Not all of the mosques were destroyed, but when they were "rebuilt", the Isabelline Gothic architecture was already set in stone. From the arches to the intricate carvings, you only realize that it is not a mosque the moment you see people and animals embedded among the carvings. The bell tower attached to the cathedral used to be a minaret. It served as living proof of the various influences that Christianity and Islam has left on this royal palace.

Seville Cathedral

Seville Cathedral, otherwise known as The Cathedral of Saint Mary of the See, was constructed, just like the cathedrals in Barcelona previously mentioned, on the ruins of a destroyed mosque during the "Reconquista". It served as a trophy to brag around when someone from the parish claimed "we shall have a church of such a kind that those who see it built will think we were mad". It emboldened their resolve so much that the clerics poured their finances into building it. Almost everything was super-sized from the altar that displayed the life cycle of Jesus to the ceilings that must have reached the sky. It became a UNESCO World Heritage site by virtue of being the biggest Gothic cathedral in the world and the third largest church in the world, the size of a football field.

Plaza de Toros de la Maestranza

The first thing that fans of the renowned opera "Carmen" remember, the Plaza de Toros de la Maestranza de Caballeria de Sevilla is one of the most recognizable stadiums in the world. It serves as a concrete proof of how bullfighting is still the most viewed spectacle in Seville. So much that men and women would even dress the part of avid fans waiting for the heroic "matador" to tame the bull. Peak season reaches feverish levels not only because of the scorching summer heat but also of the troves of tourists that flock the bullring during Feria de Abril (April Fair).

Where to Eat in Seville

Let's look at some of the best places to eat close to Basilica Macarena like El Rincon de Rosita. Some of the best homegrown dishes are found here. When appetizers like fresh bacalao give you that feeling that you have found your Spanish comfort food, wait until you get to try anchoas y tomate - literally fish and tomatoes an toasted bread. Expect a lot of Mediterranean dishes here since Seville's by the coast after all. In case you'd like to keep it Spanish without eating seafood, there is a dish called Bull's Tails covered in brothy sauce and served with potato fries. Of course, don't leave this restaurant without trying their paella.

Before you think that only pork can be turned to tapas, pop into La Cantina Restaurant for some seafood tapas. While red meat alternatives are available on the menu, most of their best sellers are still the seafood items like the aforementioned seafood tapas and clams.

If you're in the mood for home-made vegetarian pitas, try Pitacasso. Yes, this is inspired by their great artist, Pablo Picasso, with the artistry diverted to Spanish cuisine. This is where you go to go as casual as you could to enjoy your sandwiches. It is more about the food and less about the ambiance and is nice and laid back.

La Gorda te da de Comer is basically what its name in Spanish suggests - a place for you to get fat. Tapas, appetizers and main course dishes are found here as well as breakfast where you can try toasted bread with bacon topped with melted cheese. You can tell the dishes are local the moment you try the tapas containing beef and venison which is what makes this restaurant unique from most restaurants - the varieties of meat used as tapas. Potatoes are also a staple. Either served as fried or topped in mojo sauce, they complement most meat dishes served here.

Chapter VII: Festivals and Events

Las Fallas de Valencia

Las Fallas de Valencia is one of the festivals that makes Valencia an even hotter place for partying. The locals still occasionally refer it to its original festival name - St. Joseph's Day, commemorated every March 19. The Fallas, or large monument effigies, referred to in the festival name, are first paraded during the day and burned in the evening. The burning part is why these effigies earned the nickname "fallas" (singular: falla) which means "torch in Latin. The funds needed to make the fallas are raised through dinners featuring the city's official dish, paella.

The effigies built will depend on the theme for that year. This gives some artists an opportunity to create parodies of public figures and shows that Spanish artistry is not limited on canvas. Since these effigies will be torched anyway, might as well create them in the image and likeness of personalities lampooned.

There are also years where a fusion of themes occur. Going with the conventional themes like fairy tales would be to attract the kid-friendly crowd. But occasionally political references still find their way into the floats. It is their way of keeping the event interesting and worth talking about.

Semana Santa

Semana Santa almost literally translates to "Holy Week" and is commemorated in Seville through processions parading floats. The floats are carried by local parishioners called "costaleros" around town. These floats featured chapters or scenes from the Passion of the Christ. While not as bloody as the film of the same name, it presented a way for the locals to remember annually the sacrifices that Christ has done for them.

The kind of euphoria and devotion seen at these processions sparks the curiosity of tourists traveling to Seville during Semana Santa. With elaborately designed floats, this religious commemoration has turned into a spectacle that the locals are proud to offer to the world.

Feria de Abril

Feria de Abril (April Fair) is celebrated on a date that depends on the date Semana Santa is commemorated. The start of the April Fair is declared official the moment midnight strikes half a month after Semana Santa. The two-week cycle doesn't always mean the fair will fall in April however, and often occurs the first week of May.

The April Fair is a convenient excuse for the women to dress up and host parties in tents called "casetas". It's also an opportunity for them to dress like flamenco dancers and host parties. The sound of castanets and hands clapping reverberate through the walls of the tent as guitarists strum vigorously to the tune of flamenco music. Tourists should note that casetas are usually an RSVP affair. Of course, this fact only sparks the curiosity of tourists, making the parties "must-see" events if you're lucky enough to get on the invitation list.

Running of the Bulls

Originally a feast to commemorate the feast day of St. Fermin, the annual Running of the Bulls became an annual event for tourists to watch. It is quite scary at first glance but participants prepare for this race seriously and they arrive at the square hours before the bulls are released.

Celebrated writer Ernest Hemingway wrote about the Running of the Bulls as a spectacle worth seeing as mentioned in his book "The Sun Also Rises". In that novel, he described it as a race with two kinds of participants - one that ran on all fours and one that ran on all twos.

Media coverage is abundant from the time the runners are dressed up until the horn is blowed, signaling the release of the bulls, and after any injuries or casualties occur, in case it happens. The runners wear white shirts and trousers with bright red bandanas tied on their necks as is tradition. It is also the organizers' way of telling the runners apart from the spectators. Most spectators wear a bandana in solidarity with the occasion but don't wear all white.

La Tomatina

If most Spaniards enjoy watching bullfights, there are Spaniards that enjoy getting into fights themselves. I am referring to La Tomatina tomato fight. It is a mock fight held every last Wednesday of August every year in Valencia. People flock to this city to join in on the fun, as outrageous as it might be. If you don't feel like having your best outfit messed up with saucy pulp, wear something that you don't mind getting tomato all over.

The origin of this riot-themed festival is the riot that occurred involving a participant that fell off his float in the middle of a parade. The float toppled because of some young folks that joined the parade got ahead of themselves due to excitement and ended up bumping to the float, knocking off one of the persons on it. The person that fell was so mad that he ended up throwing whatever he could get his hands on to anyone that he saw. Everyone that got hit retaliated by throwing vegetables from the stalls close to the parade. The cops had to interfere just to stop them. People got arrested but the young folks that got hit never forgot. A year after, the same folks involved did it again. But instead of pestering somebody's vegetable stall, they brought their own tomatoes. Again, the police came. People got arrested. It just keeps happening on an annual basis. The authorities then made the "festival" official and eventually set the rules to keep the memory of this, um, event. The most obvious change would be the tomatoes used in the mock fight are the ones too rotten to put on your plate.

Public showers are available on site. Just expect the lines to be long though as this is one of the jam-packed events where even foreigners participate. Learning basic Spanish is a must so in case of emergency, you can correctly express the help you need.

This is a mock fight after all and here are the rules (rephrased):

No bottles. Even plastic bottles hurt so don't bother.

No t-shirts. No wonder a most of the participants are males.

Crush the tomatoes before throwing. This is a mock fight after all so getting hurt should be avoided on both the throwers and those that get hit.

Avoid the trucks containing the tomatoes. Self-explanatory. Don't get hit by the trucks.

Stop upon hearing the 2nd banger. As cathartic as throwing things may seem, this is still a mock fight. So know when to stop.

See You In Spain!

We hope that you found this travel guide to Spain helpful as you plan your trip. Have a fun, safe journey or as they say in Spain, "Buen viaje"!

Experience Everything Travel Guide Collection™

www.ingramcontent.com/pod-product-compliance
Lightning Source LLC
Chambersburg PA
CBHW071752020426
42331CB00008B/2281